— Journal —

My
*S*piritual
Inheritance

Juanita Bynum

Charisma
HOUSE
A STRANG COMPANY

Most STRANG COMMUNICATIONS/CHARISMA HOUSE/SILOAM products are available at special quantity discounts for bulk purchase for sales promotions, premiums, fund-raising, and educational needs. For details, write Strang Communications/Charisma House/Siloam, 600 Rinehart Road, Lake Mary, Florida 32746, or telephone (407) 333-0600.

MY SPIRITUAL INHERITANCE JOURNAL by Juanita Bynum
Published by Charisma House
A Strang Company
600 Rinehart Road
Lake Mary, Florida 32746
www.charismahouse.com

Unless otherwise noted, all Scripture quotations are from the Amplified Bible. Old Testament copyright © 1965, 1987 by the Zondervan Corporation. The Amplified New Testament copyright © 1954, 1958, 1987 by the Lockman Foundation. Used by permission.

Scripture quotations marked KJV are from the King James Version of the Bible.

Cover design by Judith McKittrick
Interior design by Terry Clifton

Library of Congress Catalog Card Number: 2004107838
International Standard Book Number: 1-59185-634-5

04 05 06 07 08 — 987654321
Printed in the United States of America

CONTENTS

INTRODUCTION

*E*verywhere I go, I see the onset of a mighty revival across this nation. People everywhere are being embraced and ushered into the body of Christ. Perhaps you are one of these people. Or perhaps you are seeking to discover more of your own spiritual inheritance. Maybe you are a mature Christian who is mentoring other Christians as a spiritual parent. Whatever the reason you are reading *My Spiritual Inheritance* and beginning to use this journal, I believe that you will be greatly blessed by writing down the revelations from God and the personal thoughts you have as you contemplate my message on receiving your spiritual inheritance. May God bless you richly as you move forward toward your spiritual destiny.

*U*se this journal to write down your personal reflections and the revelation that comes to you from reading *My Spiritual Inheritance*. May God move you into your spiritual destiny from reading my book.

_____

_____

_____

_____

_____

_____

_____

_____

_____

_____

_____

THE VOICE OF THE FATHER

_____

_____

_____

_____

_____

_____

_____

_____

_____

_____

_____

_____

_____

_____

_____

_____

_____

_____

_____

_____

_____

_____

_____

_____

_____

_____

_____

No matter what you may have missed in life, what you may have, or what you desire for your future—the ultimate desire of the Lord is for you to experience true spiritual fatherhood.

But solid food is for full-grown men, for those whose senses and mental faculties are trained by practice to discriminate and distinguish between what is morally good and noble and what is evil and contrary either to divine or human law.

—HEBREWS 5:14

_____

_____

_____

_____

_____

_____

_____

_____

_____

_____

_____

_____

_____

_____

_____

_____

_____

_____

_____

_____

_____

_____

_____

_____

_____

_____

Any place where you are not receiving the manifold blessings of God is your spiritual Egypt.

I BROUGHT YOU
INTO A PLENTIFUL
LAND TO ENJOY
ITS FRUITS AND
GOOD THINGS.
—JEREMIAH 2:7

_____

_____

_____

_____

_____

_____

_____

_____

_____

_____

_____

_____

_____

_____

If you have received
Jesus and are still
going through
that wilderness
experience, be
confident that you
belong to God. If He
is your heavenly
Father, God will
make sure you
receive His portion.

THE POWER OF OBEDIENCE

_____

_____

_____

_____

_____

_____

_____

_____

_____

_____

_____

_____

_____

_____

_____

_____

_____

_____

_____

_____

_____

_____

_____

_____

_____

One of the first signs that you are in the right spiritual home is when your spirit becomes humbled to the point that you ask, "What can I do?"

*F*or by the grace (unmerited favor of God) given to me I warn everyone among you not to estimate and think of himself more highly than he ought [not to have an exaggerated opinion of his own importance], but to rate his ability with sober judgment, each according to the degree of faith apportioned by God to him.

—ROMANS 12:3

_____

_____

_____

_____

_____

_____

_____

_____

_____

_____

_____

_____

_____

_____

_____

_____

_____

_____

_____

_____

_____

_____

_____

True sons and daughters in the kingdom are focused on the will and vision of their spiritual fathers.

When everything is subjected to Him, then the Son Himself will also subject Himself to [the Father] Who put all things under Him, so that God may be all in all [be everything to everyone, supreme, the indwelling and controlling factor of life].

—1 Corinthians 15:28

_____

_____

_____

_____

_____

_____

_____

_____

_____

_____

_____

_____

The way we obtain
the respect of
having a ministry
is by being faithful
to that which
belongs to our
spiritual father.

RECEIVING THE FATHER'S PORTION

_____

_____

_____

_____

_____

_____

_____

_____

_____

_____

_____

_____

_____

_____

_____

_____

_____

_____

_____

_____

_____

_____

_____

_____

*W*hen you come into the knowledge of your spiritual parents, you will come with a vision, a goal, and a desire— but they are going to give you destiny.

*H*e who is faithful in a very little [thing] is faithful also in much, and he who is dishonest and unjust in a very little [thing] is dishonest and unjust also in much.

—LUKE 16:10

_____

_____

_____

_____

_____

_____

_____

_____

_____

_____

_____

_____

_____

_____

_____

_____

_____

_____

_____

_____

_____

_____

_____

_____

God has introduced you to a spiritual father so that
through him the Lord can draw you into destiny.

GIVING THANKS TO
THE FATHER, WHO
HAS QUALIFIED AND
MADE US FIT TO
SHARE THE POR-
TION WHICH IS THE
INHERITANCE OF
THE SAINTS (GOD'S
HOLY PEOPLE)
IN THE LIGHT.
—COLOSSIANS 1:12

_____

_____

_____

_____

_____

_____

_____

_____

_____

_____

_____

_____

_____

_____

_____

_____

_____

_____

_____

_____

_____

_____

_____

_____

_____

_____

_____

You will never
get to your next
level until you are
willing to give up
those who think
you are wonderful
in order to stand
in the presence
of somebody
who can discern
what you need.

THE ANOINTING: DIVINE ORDER

_____

_____

_____

_____

_____

_____

_____

_____

_____

_____

_____

_____

_____

_____

_____

_____

_____

_____

_____

_____

_____

_____

_____

_____

_____

_____

_____

hen you truly meet your divine connection, that person will have the anointing to help resolve your past while ushering you into the future.

*T*hen the Spirit of the Lord will come upon you mightily, and you will show yourself to be a prophet with them; and you will be turned into another man.

—1 SAMUEL 10:6

_____

_____

_____

_____

_____

_____

_____

_____

_____

_____

_____

_____

_____

_____

_____

_____

_____

_____

_____

_____

_____

_____

_____

_____

_____

*R*egardless of the circumstances, it is your leader's responsibility to make an announcement about you.

Do not boast of [yourself and] tomorrow, for you know not what a day may bring forth. Let another man praise you, and not your own mouth; a stranger, and not your own lips.

—Proverbs 27:1–2

_____

_____

_____

_____

_____

_____

_____

_____

_____

_____

_____

_____

_____

_____

_____

Your
divine purpose
can only be
established
by counsel.

STEPPING OVER AUTHORITY

_____

_____

_____

_____

_____

_____

_____

_____

_____

_____

_____

_____

_____

_____

_____

_____

_____

_____

_____

_____

_____

_____

_____

_____

_____

_____

_____

_____

*B*ecause of His submission to God, Jesus had access to everything that belonged to the Father.

Although He was a Son, He learned [active, special] obedience through what He suffered.

—HEBREWS 5:8

_____

_____

_____

_____

_____

_____

_____

_____

_____

_____

_____

_____

_____

_____

_____

_____

_____

_____

_____

_____

_____

_____

_____

_____

_____

eople have made submission a matter of submission to *a person* and have not understood that submission is a matter of submitting to *the authority of God*.

HAS THE LORD
AS GREAT A DE-
LIGHT IN BURNT
OFFERINGS AND
SACRIFICES AS IN
OBEYING THE VOICE
OF THE LORD?
BEHOLD, TO OBEY
IS BETTER THAN
SACRIFICE, AND TO
HEARKEN THAN
THE FAT OF RAMS.
—1 SAMUEL 15:22

_____

_____

_____

_____

_____

_____

_____

_____

_____

_____

_____

_____

_____

_____

God doesn't get
the glory until
we are walking
in obedience to
what He says.

The Generational Curse

_____

_____

_____

_____

_____

_____

_____

_____

_____

_____

_____

_____

_____

_____

_____

_____

_____

_____

_____

_____

_____

_____

_____

_____

When leaders have a spirit of pride, it causes them to dis-
obey the Word of the Lord, either because of the mighti-
ness of their ministries or the strength of their talents
and callings in God.

*Y*ou shall not bow down yourself to them or serve them; for I the Lord your God am a jealous God, visiting the iniquity of the fathers upon the children to the third and fourth generation of those who hate Me, but showing mercy and steadfast love to a thousand generations of those who love Me and keep My commandments.

—EXODUS 20:5–6

_____

_____

_____

_____

_____

_____

_____

_____

_____

_____

_____

_____

_____

_____

_____

_____

_____

_____

_____

_____

_____

_____

_____

_____

_____

_____

When you become so great in your own eyes that you think you can operate in a spiritual office God hasn't anointed and appointed you for, you are putting yourself in a dangerous position.

THEREFORE, I WILL
ALL THE MORE
GLADLY GLORY IN
MY WEAKNESSES
AND INFIRMI-
TIES, THAT THE
STRENGTH AND
POWER OF CHRIST
(THE MESSIAH)
MAY REST (YES,
MAY PITCH A
TENT OVER AND
DWELL) UPON ME!
—2 CORINTHIANS
12:9

_____

_____

_____

_____

_____

_____

_____

_____

_____

_____

_____

_____

_____

_____

_____

_____

_____

_____

_____

_____

_____

_____

_____

_____

_____

_____

_____

_____

This is how
greatness is birthed:
the portion already
within you balanced
with the portion
you inherit from
your spiritual father.

THE POWER OF REBUKE

_____

_____

_____

_____

_____

_____

_____

_____

_____

_____

_____

hen God puts you in the position to be rebuked, whether it's for something you have said, done, felt, or believed, He is announcing to you that He loves you.

he ear that listens to reproof [that leads to or gives] life will remain among the wise. He who refuses and ignores instruction and correction despises himself, but he who heeds reproof gets understanding. The reverent and worshipful fear of the Lord brings instruction in Wisdom, and humility comes before honor.

—Proverbs 15:31–33

_____

_____

_____

_____

_____

_____

_____

_____

_____

_____

_____

_____

_____

_____

_____

_____

_____

_____

_____

_____

_____

_____

_____

*Y*our spiritual leaders need to carve character in you to bring you to the level where you can handle the word you received.

THOSE WHOM
I [DEARLY AND
TENDERLY] LOVE, I
TELL THEIR FAULTS
AND CONVICT AND
CONVINCE AND
REPROVE AND
CHASTEN [I DIS-
CIPLINE AND IN-
STRUCT THEM]. SO
BE ENTHUSIASTIC
AND IN EARNEST
AND BURNING
WITH ZEAL AND
REPENT [CHANG-
ING YOUR MIND
AND ATTITUDE].
—REVELATION 3:19

es and plans are established by counsel.

—Proverbs 20:18

_____

_____

_____

_____

_____

_____

_____

_____

_____

_____

_____

God's process is
to correct, train,
and bless you now
so that when you
come into destiny,
God doesn't have to
correct and train
you nearly as much.

THE ABSENCE OF CORRECTION

_____

_____

_____

_____

_____

_____

_____

_____

_____

_____

_____

_____

_____

_____

_____

_____

_____

_____

_____

_____

_____

_____

_____

_____

_____

_____

Rebuke is absolutel
strength, for those wh
their lives.

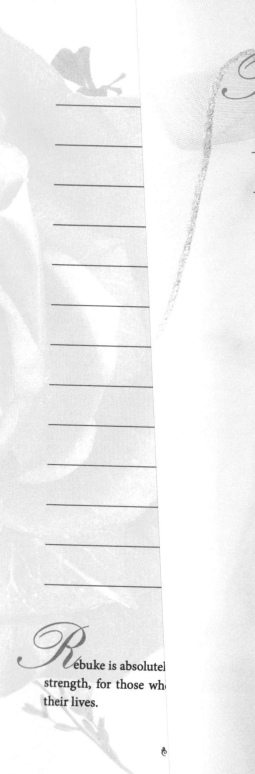

Purpos

_____

_____

_____

_____

_____

_____

_____

_____

_____

_____

_____

_____

_____

_____

Rebuke...godly correction...is part of God's preparation of His children for their spiritual inheritance.

A GOOD NAME IS
RATHER TO BE
CHOSEN THAN
GREAT RICHES.
—PROVERBS 22:1

_____

_____

_____

_____

_____

_____

_____

_____

_____

_____

_____

_____

_____

_____

_____

_____

_____

_____

_____

_____

_____

_____

_____

_____

_____

_____

_____

_____

_____

_____

_____

_____

God can use you
even when you are
wrong...but be
careful...you could
be working for the
kingdom while on
your way to hell.

THE SPIRIT OF TRUTH

_____

_____

_____

_____

_____

_____

_____

_____

_____

_____

_____

_____

_____

_____

_____

_____

_____

_____

_____

_____

_____

_____

_____

_____

_____

_____

_____

_____

_Y_our call must be directed, confirmed, and proven by the Word of Truth—that is how you know you belong to God.

*E*very Scripture is God-breathed (given by His inspiration) and profitable for instruction, for reproof and conviction of sin, for correction of error and discipline in obedience, [and] for training in righteousness...so that the man of God may be complete and proficient, well fitted and thoroughly equipped for every good work.

—2 TIMOTHY 3:16–17

_____

_____

_____

_____

_____

_____

_____

_____

_____

_____

_____

_____

_____

_____

_____

_____

_____

_____

_____

_____

_____

_____

_____

_____

If you can't handle the weight of temptation in your own spirit, you will never be able to handle the weight of the anointing for anyone else.

FOR THE TIME BE-
ING NO DISCIPLINE
BRINGS JOY, BUT
SEEMS GRIEVOUS
AND PAINFUL; BUT
AFTERWARDS IT
YIELDS A PEACE-
ABLE FRUIT OF
RIGHTEOUSNESS TO
THOSE WHO HAVE
BEEN TRAINED
BY IT [A HARVEST
OF FRUIT WHICH
CONSISTS IN
RIGHTEOUSNESS—
IN CONFORMITY
TO GOD'S WILL IN
PURPOSE, THOUGHT,
AND ACTION, RESULT-
ING IN RIGHT LIVING
AND RIGHT STAND-
ING WITH GOD].
    —HEBREWS 12:11

_____

_____

_____

_____

_____

_____

_____

_____

_____

_____

_____

_____

_____

_____

_____

Don't be satisfied
with junk food,
cookies, candy,
and prophecies.
Hunger and thirst
for the presence of
God in your life. In
order to activate
your spiritual
inheritance, you
must learn to
embrace the
Spirit of Truth.

THE MAKING OF A SON

_____

_____

_____

_____

_____

_____

_____

_____

_____

_____

_____

_____

_____

_____

_____

_____

_____

_____

_____

_____

_____

_____

_____

_____

ubmission in the course of a relationship between a spiritual parent and a son or daughter is very powerful. We must learn to recognize that the bonds of spiritual relationship are strengthened by the process of walking through both good—and bad—with that person.

For all who are led by the Spirit of God are sons of God.

—ROMANS 8:14

_____

_____

_____

_____

_____

_____

_____

_____

_____

_____

_____

_____

_____

_____

_____

_____

_____

_____

_____

_____

_____

_____

_____

_____

*W*hen you see your spiritual leaders going through something, that's your opportunity to get in your anointing—
because that's what ministers to them.

AND IT CAME TO
PASS AFTERWARD,
THAT DAVID'S
HEART SMOTE HIM,
BECAUSE HE HAD
CUT OFF SAUL'S
SKIRT. AND HE
SAID UNTO HIS MEN,
THE LORD FORBID
THAT I SHOULD DO
THIS THING UNTO
MY MASTER, THE
LORD'S ANOINTED,
TO STRETCH
FORTH MINE
HAND AGAINST
HIM, SEEING HE
IS THE ANOINTED
OF THE LORD.
—1 SAMUEL
24:5–6, KJV

_____

_____

_____

_____

_____

_____

_____

_____

_____

_____

_____

_____

_____

_____

If you will stay
under the covering
of obedience,
you will be
demonstrating to
God that you are
ready to stand the
test of real spiritual
sonship, and you
will become a real
son or daughter.

THE SEDUCTION OF JEZEBEL

_____

_____

_____

_____

_____

_____

_____

_____

_____

_____

_____

The spirit of Jezebel intends to frustrate the plans of our heavenly Father, to wreak havoc in the church, and to stop His purposes.

*B*ut I have this against you: that you tolerate the woman Jezebel...who is teaching and leading astray my servants....Take note: I will throw her on a bed [of anguish], and those who commit adultery with her [her paramours] I will bring down to pressing distress and severe affliction.

—REVELATION 2:20–22

_____

_____

_____

_____

_____

_____

_____

_____

_____

_____

_____

_____

_____

_____

_____

_____

_____

_____

_____

_____

_____

Jezebel cannot rule where she hasn't been given authority. But she will assume authority through anyone—male or female, Jew or Gentile, minister or lay person—who gives her that place.

WHOEVER WISHES
TO BE GREAT
AMONG YOU MUST
BE YOUR SERVANT,
AND WHOEVER DE-
SIRES TO BE FIRST
AMONG YOU MUST
BE YOUR SLAVE—
JUST AS THE SON OF
MAN CAME NOT TO
BE WAITED ON BUT
TO SERVE, AND TO
GIVE HIS LIFE AS A
RANSOM FOR MANY
[THE PRICE PAID TO
SET THEM FREE].
—MATTHEW
20:26–28

_____

_____

_____

_____

_____

_____

_____

_____

_____

_____

_____

_____

_____

The church isn't about seats or activities or personalities. It's not about you; it's not about me—it's much bigger than any one person. The Father's portion is about souls.

BABYLON'S FALL

_____

_____

_____

_____

_____

_____

_____

_____

_____

_____

_____

_____

_____

_____

_____

_____

_____

_____

_____

_____

_____

_____

_____

_____

_____

_____

*B*elievers are chasing demon spirits and binding "symptoms," but our real enemy is Babylon—their demonic stronghold.

And he shouted with a mighty voice, She is fallen! She has become a resort and dwelling place for demons, a dungeon haunted by every loathsome spirit, an abode for every filthy and detestable bird.

—REVELATION 18:2

_____

_____

_____

_____

_____

_____

_____

_____

_____

_____

_____

_____

_____

_____

_____

_____

_____

_____

_____

_____

_____

_____

On every level, this spirit has tried to copycat the order of the Lord. But in the end, just like the beast on which she rides, Babylon will be consumed with fire.

O LORD OF HOST,
BLESSED (HAPPY,
FORTUNATE, TO
BE ENVIED) IS THE
MAN WHO TRUSTS
IN YOU [LEANING,
AND BELIEVING ON
YOU, COMMITTING
ALL AND CONFI-
DENTLY LOOKING
TO YOU, AND THAT
WITHOUT FEAR OR
MISGIVING]! LORD,
YOU HAVE [AT LAST]
BEEN FAVORABLE
AND HAVE DEALT
GRACIOUSLY WITH
YOUR LAND [OF
CANAAN]; YOU
HAVE BROUGHT
BACK [FROM
BABYLON] THE CAP-
TIVES OF JACOB.
—PSALM 84:12–85:1

_____

_____

_____

_____

_____

_____

_____

_____

_____

_____

_____

_____

_____

It is time to rise
up and take what
rightfully belongs
to us! We must keep
moving forward,
with the Lord Jesus
Christ; no weapon
formed against
us shall prosper.

THE REAL AUTHORITY

_____

_____

_____

_____

_____

_____

_____

_____

_____

_____

_____

_____

_____

_____

_____

_____

_____

_____

_____

_____

_____

_____

_____

When you yield your life to God, He will throw the authority of Jezebel down. It is a *life* that throws her down—not *talk*.

*I*t was the will of the Lord to bruise Him; He has put Him to grief and made Him sick. When You and He make His life an offering for sin [and He has risen from the dead, in time to come], He shall see His [spiritual] offspring. He shall prolong His days, and the will and pleasure of the Lord shall prosper in His hand.

—Isaiah 53:10

_____

_____

_____

_____

_____

_____

_____

_____

_____

_____

_____

_____

_____

_____

_____

_____

_____

_____

_____

_____

_____

_____

*W*hen everything you know is being tested and tried, will you still stand and say, "Nevertheless, I will do my Father's will"?

ALL AUTHORITY
(ALL POWER OF
RULE) IN HEAVEN
AND ON EARTH HAS
BEEN GIVEN TO ME.
—MATTHEW 28:18

_____

_____

_____

_____

_____

_____

_____

_____

_____

_____

_____

_____

We must become
yielded vessels
unto God because
the authority of
God through the
anointing defeats
the enemy.

OUR TRUE INHERITANCE

_____

_____

_____

_____

_____

_____

_____

_____

_____

_____

_____

_____

_____

_____

_____

_____

_____

_____

_____

_____

_____

_____

_____

*I*f you open the "gate" of your life to the enemy, he will trample everything under his feet and then try to take you out.

*B*ehold, I am laying in Zion for a foundation, a Stone, a tested Stone, a precious Cornerstone of sure foundation; he who believes (trusts in, relies on, and adheres to that Stone) will not be ashamed or give way or hasten away [in sudden panic]....The stone which the builders rejected has become the chief cornerstone.

—ISAIAH 28:16; PSALM 118:22

_____

_____

_____

_____

_____

_____

_____

_____

_____

_____

_____

_____

_____

_____

_____

_____

_____

_____

_____

_____

_____

_____

Unless we remain submitted to God and to those in positions of divine authority, the anointing to break every yoke and reestablish our spiritual foundation will be hindered.

To Him Who ever
loves us and has
once [for all]
loosed and freed
us from our sins
by His own blood,
and formed us
into a kingdom
(a royal race),
priests to His God
and Father—to
Him be the glory
and the power
and the majesty
and the domin-
ion throughout
the ages and
forever and ever.
Amen (so be it).
—Revelation 1:5–6

_____

_____

_____

_____

_____

_____

_____

_____

_____

_____

_____

_____

_____

Our true inheritance—the supernatural character of our Father through Jesus Christ and the ministry of the Holy Spirit—is waiting to be restored to us in the house of our spiritual father.

IT'S TIME TO REBUILD

_____

_____

_____

_____

_____

_____

_____

_____

_____

_____

_____

_____

_____

_____

_____

_____

_____

_____

_____

_____

_____

_____

_____

_____

_____

_____

*B*elievers are chasing demon spirits and binding "symptoms," but our real enemy is Babylon—their demonic stronghold.

When a man's ways please the Lord, He makes even his
enemies to be at peace with him.

—PROVERBS 16:7

_____

_____

_____

_____

_____

_____

_____

_____

_____

_____

_____

_____

_____

_____

*I*t is time to rise up and take what rightfully belongs to us!

Closing
Prayer

Dear heavenly Father, thank You for revealing the truth about my spiritual inheritance. Forgive me for the times that I have removed myself from Your covering by either disobeying Your Word or failing to acknowledge the counsel of my spiritual parents. I now know that in their counsel I will find true riches.

Father, I acknowledge my sin; cleanse me from all unrighteousness, and help me to become a true son or daughter of the gospel in this final hour. Create in me a clean heart, and renew a right spirit within me. Thank You, Lord, that I can hear Your voice, obey the counsel of Your Word, and activate the full measure of faith You have placed in my spirit. From this day forward, I thank You for helping me to become a true servant in Your kingdom. Amen.

Strang Communications, the publisher of both Charisma House and *Charisma* magazine, wants to give you a FREE SUBSCRIPTION to our award-winning magazine.

Since its inception in 1975, *Charisma* magazine has helped thousands of Christians stay connected with what God is doing worldwide.

Within its pages you will discover in-depth reports and the latest news from a Christian perspective, biblical health tips, global events in the body of Christ, personality profiles, and so much more. Join the family of *Charisma* readers who enjoy feeding their spirit each month with miracle-filled testimonies and inspiring articles that bring clarity, provoke prayer, and demand answers.

To claim your **3 free issues** of *Charisma,* send your name and address to: Charisma 3 Free Issue Offer, 600 Rinehart Road, Lake Mary, FL 32746. Or you may call 1-800-829-3346 and ask for Offer # 93FREE. This offer is only valid in the USA.

---

www.charismamag.com